ROOMS TO RICHES

ROOMS TO RICHES

The Complete Blueprint for Generating $3,000–8,000+ Per Month in Shared Housing Income Without Owning a Single Property

For permissions requests, contact:
beacons.ai/kjoyner

Print ISBN: 978-0-9979557-2-9
eBook ISBN: 978-0-9979557-3-6
Audiobook ISBN: 978-0-9979557-4-3

Published by Kelly Joyner
Charlotte, North Carolina
United States of America

First Edition

Printed in the United States of America

Disclaimer: This book is for informational and educational purposes only and does not constitute legal, financial, tax, or investment advice. Consult qualified professionals before making any business or investment decisions. The author and publisher disclaim any liability arising from use of this material.

ROOMS TO RICHES

The Complete Blueprint for Generating $3,000–8,000+ Per Month

in Shared Housing Income Without Owning a Single Property

Kelly Janine Joyner

Kelly Joyner

For all the women in my life who pushed, encouraged, and never let me quit.

And for the woman reading this who has given everything to everyone else and is finally ready to build something for herself.

You are not too late. You are right on time.

Table of Contents

Introduction: Why This Book Exists — And Why Now Is Your Moment

Let's be honest with each other right from the start.

You didn't pick up this book because life is going perfectly. You picked it up because something isn't adding up — the income, the savings, the retirement plan that may not exist yet, or the nagging feeling that there has to be a way to generate real money without waiting another twenty years.

Maybe you've watched other people talk about real estate investing and assumed it wasn't for you. Maybe you assumed you needed a huge down payment, a perfect credit score, or some kind of insider knowledge to even get started.

I understand. And I'm here to tell you: this model — shared housing through rental arbitrage — was practically built for exactly where you are right now.

You don't need to buy property. You don't need a mortgage. You don't need perfect credit. What you need is the ability to find a house, rent it from a landlord, furnish it thoughtfully, and rent out individual rooms to people who desperately need them. The difference between what you pay the landlord and what your tenants pay you is your income.

This updated edition includes everything from the original — plus a brand new Housing Models Defined section, a complete Bonus Chapter on the Reentry Housing Model, an expanded glossary, and updated FAQ sections throughout.

By the time you finish this book, you won't be wondering if this is possible. You'll be wondering why nobody told you about this sooner.

Let's get started.

COACH TIP

Read this book with a notebook next to you. When something gives you an idea for your market, write it down immediately. By the time you finish the last chapter, you'll have the beginning of your actual business plan already started.

Real Estate Terms — Explained Like a Friend

Before we go any further, let's make sure we're speaking the same language. Here's what you actually need to know, explained the way a good friend would explain it over coffee.

Rental Arbitrage
You rent a property from a landlord and then rent it out to other people at a higher combined total. You keep the difference.
Example: You rent a 5-bedroom house for $2,000/month. You rent each room for $600. After expenses, you pocket the profit.

Subletting / Subleasing
When you rent a property and then rent all or part of it to someone else. Always do this with the landlord's written knowledge and permission.
Example: You sign the lease with the landlord. You then rent individual rooms to five different people.

Living Agreement
Used in sober living and transitional homes — a program participation agreement, not a lease. Creates a program operator-participant relationship providing significant legal protection.
Example: Your sober living resident signs a living agreement stating their continued residence depends on following program rules.

Program Fee
In sober living and transitional homes, you collect program fees — not rent. The language matters legally.
Example: Your sober living resident pays an $850/month program fee for participation in your structured recovery housing program.

Cash Flow
The money left over after you've paid all your expenses. Positive cash flow means you're making money.

> Example: Total income $3,200/month minus total expenses $2,500/month equals $700/month cash flow.

House Manager
A trusted person who handles day-to-day operations. Common in sober living and transitional homes. Typically receives reduced fees plus a small stipend.
Example: Your House Manager lives in the sober living home, enforces curfews, and facilitates house meetings.

SSI / SSDI
Government programs providing monthly payments to people with disabilities or very low income. Many shared housing tenants receive these.
Example: Your tenant receives $943/month from SSI. Your room at $550/month, utilities included, fits within their budget.

Recidivism
The tendency of a previously incarcerated person to reoffend. Stable housing is one of the strongest protective factors against recidivism.
Example: Studies show people with stable housing in the first 72 hours after release have dramatically lower recidivism rates.

NARR

National Alliance for Recovery Residences — sets quality standards for sober living homes.

Example: Pursuing NARR certification signals quality to referral partners and may open doors to state funding.

Fair Chance Housing

Laws restricting landlords from automatically disqualifying applicants based on criminal history. Important for reentry housing operators.

Example: Seattle's fair chance housing law limits when and how landlords can use criminal background information.

Zoning

Rules set by local governments that determine how land and buildings can be used.

Example: In your city, a residential zone allows no more than four unrelated adults per household.

Vacancy

A room or bed that's empty and not generating income. Every vacant room is money you're not making.

Example: You have 4 rooms. One is vacant this month. That empty room costs you $650 in lost income.

Housing Models Defined: Know What You're Building Before You Build It

One of the most common sources of confusion for new shared housing providers is the terminology. Each model is distinct — with its own legal framework, tenant population, income range, and operational requirements.

The Six Models — Defined

Licensed Group Home

TYPE: Clinical Care Facility — State Regulated

What It Is:
A licensed group home provides professional care and support services requiring clinical oversight. Licensed by a state agency with specific staffing and documentation requirements.

Legal Consideration:
Requires state licensing. This is NOT what we teach in this book.

Income Range:
Varies — often subsidized by state contracts. Not applicable to our model.

In Plain English:
Think: a small residential medical facility. You are providing clinical care, not just housing.

Unlicensed Group Home

TYPE: Residential Housing — No Clinical License Required

What It Is:
A shared residential property where self-sufficient adults live together with house structure and rules — without state clinical licensing or medical oversight.

Legal Consideration:
No state clinical license required. Governed by standard landlord-tenant law and occupancy rules.

Income Range:
$700–$1,400 net per month.

In Plain English:
Think: a well-managed shared household with clear rules. You provide the house and framework.

Transitional Housing

TYPE: Structured Temporary Housing — Program Based

What It Is:
Temporary, structured housing designed to help people move from a crisis situation toward stable independent living.

Legal Consideration:
No clinical license required. Operates under living agreements, not leases. Subject to local housing regulations.

Income Range:
$1,200–$2,500 net per month.

In Plain English:
Think: the runway between where someone has been and where they're going.

Rooming House

TYPE: Shared Residential Housing — General Population

What It Is:
A property where multiple adults each rent their own private room and share common spaces. No specific crisis population or clinical framework.

Legal Consideration:
Governed by standard landlord-tenant law. Residents sign sublease agreements.

Income Range:
$800–$1,800 net per month.

In Plain English:
Think: the simplest and most accessible of all shared housing models. Great for beginners.

Sober Living Home

TYPE: Recovery Housing — Program Based / Living Agreement

What It Is:

A structured, substance-free shared housing community for adults in recovery. You are not providing treatment — you are providing the environment that makes continued recovery possible.

Legal Consideration:

No clinical license required in most states. Uses living agreements — NOT leases. Federal fair housing law protects residents in recovery.

Income Range:

$3,000–$4,500 net per month.

In Plain English:

Think: transitional housing with one defining, non-negotiable rule — sobriety.

Reentry Housing

TYPE: Post-Incarceration Transitional Housing — Program Based

What It Is:

Structured transitional housing for adults coming out of incarceration. Addresses the critical 72-hour window after release.

Legal Consideration:

No clinical license required. Uses living agreements. Fair chance housing laws vary significantly by state and city.

Income Range:

$1,500–$3,000 net per month.

In Plain English:

Think: the bridge between incarceration and independent living.

Side-by-Side Comparison

Model	License?	Agreement Type	Population	Net/Month*
Licensed Group Home	YES	State contract	High support needs	Varies
Unlicensed Group Home	NO	Sublease	Self-sufficient adults	$700–$1,400

Model	License?	Agreement Type	Population	Net/Month*
Transitional Housing	NO	Living agreement	Crisis-to-stability	$1,200–$2,500
Rooming House	NO	Sublease	General adults	$800–$1,800
Sober Living Home	NO (most states)	Living agreement	Adults in recovery	$3,000–$4,500
Reentry Housing	NO	Living agreement	Post-incarceration	$1,500–$3,000

REAL TALK

These models are NOT interchangeable. The agreement type determines your legal relationship with residents. Know your model before you sign your first lease.

CHAPTER ONE

The Opportunity: Why Shared Housing Is a Hidden Goldmine

You picked up this book because something in your life is not working the way you want it to. Maybe you're working a job that pays the bills but leaves nothing left over. Maybe you're a woman over 40 who looked at her bank account and realized that retirement is coming faster than the savings are growing.

You don't have to be any of those things to profit from real estate. That's not a motivational slogan — it's the literal premise of this book.

What Is Shared Housing, Really?

At its most basic, shared housing is exactly what it sounds like. Multiple adults share a property — each having their own private sleeping space — while using common areas together. What makes it a business is the difference between renting a whole house versus renting individual rooms within it.

	Traditional Rental	Shared Housing Model
Property	5-bed house	Same 5-bed house
Monthly rent you pay	$2,200	$2,200
How rented out	Whole house, one tenant	5 rooms @ $700/room
Monthly income	$2,200	$3,500
After utilities & supplies	N/A	-$400 estimated
Monthly net profit	$0	~$900

MONEY MOVE

The real wealth in shared housing is that each property you add multiplies your income without multiplying your time by the same ratio. Your second property takes a fraction of the effort the first one did.

The Housing Demand Is Real

The demand for affordable shared housing is not a trend. Housing costs have risen dramatically in most U.S. markets while wages have not kept pace. When you step in and provide quality shared housing, you are filling a gap that is genuinely underserved.

Why You Don't Need to Own Property

Traditional real estate investing requires a down payment — typically 20% of the purchase price. Rental arbitrage requires none of that. Your startup costs are primarily the first month's rent, a security deposit, and furnishing the property — often $3,000 to $6,000.

WATCH OUT

Rental arbitrage is completely legal — the key is doing it transparently with the landlord's knowledge and written agreement. We cover exactly how to approach landlords in Chapter Five.

Who This Works Best For

This model works especially well for people who are organized, have strong people skills, can invest $3,000 to $7,000 in startup costs, and are motivated by both income and community impact. Your life experience is a business asset here.

REAL TALK

You don't have to be a natural businessperson to succeed at this. You have to be consistent, organized, and genuinely committed to running a good operation. The knowledge is in this book. The consistency is yours to bring.

A Word Before You Go...

The opportunity you just read about has been waiting for someone exactly like you. God does not waste preparation — and everything you have been through has prepared you for this.

Before you turn the page — write down one reason why YOU are the right person to build this. That reason is your foundation. Everything else gets built on top of it.

Notes

Notes

CHAPTER TWO

The Non-Licensed VA Group Home Model (2 Beds Per Room)

Let's start this chapter with a very important clarification. This model is informal shared housing for veterans and other adults on fixed incomes. It is NOT a licensed care facility. You are providing rooms in a shared house to adults who are fully capable of caring for themselves.

Who Your Tenants Are

Veterans are one of the most underserved populations in the American housing market. The VA offers housing assistance including HUD-VASH vouchers, but supply falls far short of demand. Your tenant pool also includes individuals receiving SSI or SSDI, adults in transitional situations, and low-income working adults.

COACH TIP

Build relationships with social workers, VA case managers, and community organizations early. Once you're on their radar as a reliable, ethical operator, they will send referrals to you consistently.

The 2-Beds-Per-Room Setup

The core profit engine is the 2-beds-per-room configuration. In any bedroom 120 square feet or larger, you can comfortably fit two single beds, two dressers, and sufficient walking space.

Configuration	Rooms	Beds	Rate/Bed	Monthly Gross
Standard (1 bed each)	4	4	$650	$2,600
2-bed rooms	4	8	$450	$3,600
5-bedroom house	5	10	$450	$4,500

Configuration	Rooms	Beds	Rate/Bed	Monthly Gross
Mixed model	5	8	Varies	$3,950 est.

BEGINNER MISTAKE

Charging below-market rates out of guilt. If you charge so little that your property loses money, you won't be able to maintain it. Charge a fair rate that keeps your business sustainable.

Monthly Income Breakdown

Item	Monthly Amount
Monthly rent (your lease)	-$1,900
Utilities	-$345
Supplies & maintenance reserve	-$240
8 beds x $475/bed/month	+$3,800
NET MONTHLY INCOME	$1,315

WATCH OUT

Plan your finances so you can cover lease costs for 2 months without relying on tenant income. This runway removes enormous pressure.

A Word Before You Go...

Veterans served this country faithfully. Now it is your turn to serve them — and be paid well for doing something that genuinely matters.

Before you move on — look up your local VA office contact information and write it in the notes below. That one number could fill your first property.

Notes

Notes

CHAPTER THREE

The Same-Sex Rooming House Model

The same-sex rooming house model has been around for generations. Women's boarding houses and men's rooming houses were a cornerstone of urban housing in the early twentieth century, and the model remains one of the most stable and in-demand forms of affordable shared housing today.

Why Single-Gender Housing Works So Well

Gender mixing in close-quarters living can create tension and discomfort, particularly for women who have histories of trauma or who prefer an all-female environment. By creating a single-gender environment, you reduce interpersonal friction significantly.

Women's Housing vs. Men's Housing

Women's Rooming Houses

Women's housing typically produces longer-term tenants. Women are more likely to keep shared spaces cleaner, less likely to cause property damage, and more likely to form supportive community relationships.

COACH TIP

If you're a woman running a women's rooming house, lead with that in your marketing. A woman-owned and operated safe house for women carries real weight in these communities.

Men's Rooming Houses

Men's housing tends to attract working men in transition, men in recovery programs, and seasonal workers. Men's houses require slightly firmer house rules, especially around alcohol and overnight guests.

Income Breakdown

Model	Rooms	Configuration	Monthly Rate	Gross Income
Private rooms only	4	1 bed/room	$700	$2,800
All shared rooms	4	2 beds/room	$450/bed	$3,600
Large house (6 rooms)	6	2 beds/room	$425/bed	$5,100
Mixed model	5	Varies	~$660 avg	$3,950

MONEY MOVE

Price your private rooms 30–40% higher than your per-bed shared room price. Tenants self-select into the option that matches their budget.

A Word Before You Go...

The right environment changes everything — for your residents and for your business. You have the power to create that environment starting with one house.

Decide right now — will your first home serve women or men? Write it in the notes below. A decision made is a direction set.

Notes

Notes

CHAPTER FOUR

Shared Living Space Model (General Population)

The co-living model attracts a broader, often higher-income demographic. Remote workers, travel nurses, people relocating for new jobs, graduate students, and people who actively prefer the community of shared living. These tenants CHOOSE this lifestyle – and people who choose something pay a premium.

Why People Choose Co-Living

- They want affordability without sacrificing quality
- They want flexibility – many co-living tenants don't want a 12-month lease
- They don't want to buy or move furniture
- They want community – remote work has made isolation a real problem

REAL TALK

You are not just renting rooms. You are selling an experience. The tenants choosing your property could find a cheaper room somewhere else.

Furnished vs. Unfurnished

A furnished room with high-speed internet, a quality bed, a dresser, a desk, and nice shared spaces rents for $800 to $950 per month in most markets. The difference pays for the furniture in six to twelve months and then becomes pure additional income.

Short-Term, Mid-Term, and Long-Term Stays

Short-Term (1–3 months)

The premium you can charge is the highest – often 30 to 50% more per month. Best for travel nurses, project workers, and people between housing situations.

Mid-Term (3–6 months)

The sweet spot. Near-short-term pricing with significantly less turnover. Travel nurses, contract workers, and graduate students are excellent mid-term tenants.

Long-Term (6+ months)

Provides stability and predictability. Income is consistent, management overhead is lower.

Sample Listing That Converts

SCRIPT

TITLE: Furnished Private Room | All-Inclusive | Professional Household

Looking for a clean, move-in-ready room with NO hidden costs? This is it.

YOUR ROOM: Quality furnished bedroom with bed, dresser, and desk.
INCLUDED: Electric, water, gas, and high-speed WiFi — one flat monthly rate.
SHARED: Modern kitchen, cozy living room, in-unit washer/dryer.

This is a peaceful, professional household. We screen residents carefully.
Monthly rate: $XXX | Flexible lease terms | Available [Date]
Text [number] to schedule a viewing.

A Word Before You Go...

The co-living market is growing every single day — and there is absolutely room for you in it. Your furnished room could be exactly what someone is searching for right now.

Search one furnished room listing in your city today. Write down what others are charging in the notes below. That number is your starting point.

Notes

Notes

CHAPTER FIVE

How to Do This WITHOUT Owning Property

This chapter is the one that changes everything for most people. Once you truly understand how rental arbitrage works, the barrier to entry disappears.

Finding the Right Properties

You're looking for properties with multiple bedrooms, at least two bathrooms, priced to leave enough spread. Search Zillow, Craigslist, Facebook Marketplace, and local rental platforms. Focus on houses — not apartments.

- Look for properties that have been on the market for a few weeks — landlords are more open to creative arrangements
- Drive neighborhoods and look for 'For Rent' signs on houses from private landlords
- Tell everyone you know that you're looking for a large house to lease for a professional housing business

How to Approach Landlords

SCRIPT

DURING OR AFTER THE PROPERTY TOUR:

'I run a professional shared housing operation. I lease properties, furnish them to a good standard, and rent individual rooms to pre-screened adults.

What that means for you is one reliable tenant — me — who pays rent on time every month. I'm prepared to sign a 12-to-24-month lease, pay first month and deposit upfront, and operate the property to a high standard.

The only thing I need from you is written permission to sublease individual rooms. Would you be open to talking through that arrangement?'

WATCH OUT

Never run a subletting operation without your landlord's knowledge. Standard lease agreements prohibit subletting without permission. Always operate transparently and get everything in writing.

Lease Clauses to Review

Clause to Review	What You're Looking For
Subletting/Assignment clause	Must permit subletting with landlord consent
Occupancy limits	Check how many occupants are allowed
Lease term	Negotiate for 12–24 months for stability
Rent escalation	Understand if and when rent can be raised
Maintenance responsibilities	Know what repairs are your responsibility
Termination / early exit	Understand your penalty for early exit

MONEY MOVE

Consider requiring first-month payment plus a security deposit from every tenant at move-in. This creates a financial buffer and signals commitment from your residents.

A Word Before You Go...

God has a way of opening doors that look locked from the outside. This model is that door — and you now have the key.

Write down one neighborhood in your city where you would want to operate. That neighborhood is where your first landlord conversation starts.

Notes

Notes

CHAPTER SIX

Setting Up the Property for Maximum Profit

How you set up your property determines not just how fast it fills, but how long tenants stay, how well they treat it, and how many referrals you get.

Furniture Strategy

- Facebook Marketplace: Your first stop. Furnish an entire bedroom for $150 to $300.
- IKEA: Clean, modern, durable furniture at accessible prices. Full bedroom setup $500–$700.
- Wayfair and Amazon: Good value for specific items, especially during sales.
- Estate sales and thrift stores: Excellent for common area furnishings.
- Habitat for Humanity ReStore: Kitchen appliances and fixtures at a fraction of retail cost.

MONEY MOVE

For your first property, set a per-room furniture budget of $400–$600. For a five-room property, that's $2,000–$3,000 total for bedrooms, plus $800–$1,200 for common areas.

Each Bedroom Should Include

- Bed frame — clean, solid, with slats or box spring
- Mattress — this matters more than anything else. Don't skimp here.
- Mattress cover — required for hygiene between tenants
- Dresser or wardrobe for clothing storage
- Desk and chair — essential for professional and co-living markets
- Mirror, reading lamp, curtains or blinds that provide actual privacy

- Small décor items that signal 'someone cared about this space'

BEGINNER MISTAKE

Skipping the mattress cover and curtains. These items cost less than $30 each and make a significant difference in how the room is perceived.

Systems That Run Your Property

Cleaning System

Establish a shared cleaning rotation from day one. Common areas should be on a weekly rotation among all tenants.

Maintenance System

Designate a single contact point for maintenance requests. Respond within 24 hours. Fix legitimate issues within 3 to 5 business days whenever possible.

Communication System

Create a group text or app-based message thread for household announcements. Keep it professional.

COACH TIP

Consider using an app like TenantCloud or Buildium for maintenance requests. It creates a paper trail, makes tracking easier, and signals professionalism to tenants.

A Word Before You Go...

A well-set room is a statement that someone cares — and that statement fills vacancies fast. Your attention to detail is not extra effort. It is your competitive advantage.

Write down your furniture budget for your first property right now. A number on paper is a plan. A plan becomes a property.

Notes

Notes

CHAPTER SEVEN

Marketing & Filling the Property FAST

You can set up the most beautiful shared housing property in your city, and it won't generate a single dollar until the rooms are filled. Marketing is the engine of your business. And the good news? Marketing shared housing doesn't require a big budget, a marketing degree, or years of experience.

Platform-by-Platform Strategy

Furnished Finder

For furnished and mid-term rentals, Furnished Finder is the most effective platform available. Built specifically for travel nurses and healthcare workers on short-term assignments, it attracts anyone looking for furnished accommodations for one to twelve months. List every furnished property here.

Facebook Marketplace and Facebook Groups

Facebook is your most powerful free marketing tool. Post on Marketplace with photos and your full listing description. More importantly, find local Facebook groups dedicated to housing, rooms for rent, local community, veterans, and recovery.

- Search: '[Your City] Rooms for Rent'
- Search: '[Your City] Veterans Housing'
- Search: '[Your City] Transitional Housing'
- Search: '[Your City] Affordable Housing'

Craigslist

Still one of the highest-traffic platforms for rooms and shared housing. Post in the 'Rooms & Shares' section with clear photos and a strong headline. Post a new listing every few days — older posts drop in visibility.

Local Community Outreach

The most reliable, highest-quality referrals come from local community organizations. Social workers, case managers, and program coordinators are actively looking for quality housing for their clients every single day.

- Contact your local VA office and introduce yourself as a housing provider
- Reach out to local homeless prevention agencies and transitional housing programs
- Contact recovery houses and treatment centers
- Connect with domestic violence shelters
- Introduce yourself to local churches and faith communities
- Contact local workforce development programs

COACH TIP

When you reach out to these organizations, say: 'I run a professional shared housing property specifically designed to serve [veterans / women in transition / people in recovery]. My rooms are clean, affordable, and I have a track record of working respectfully with residents in transition. I'd love to be a resource for your clients.'

Screening Tenants Properly

Filling your property fast is important. Filling it with the wrong tenants is expensive. Bad tenant decisions are the number one cause of cash flow problems, property damage, and burnout in shared housing.

- What is your current housing situation and why are you looking to move?
- What do you do for income, and can you tell me about that?
- Have you lived in shared housing before?
- What are your typical daily and evening routines?

WATCH OUT

Do not rent to anyone before completing a basic screening conversation and income verification. The 'fill it quickly' pressure is real — but moving in an unscreened tenant to fill a vacancy fast is one of the most common and expensive mistakes in this business.

Move-In Process

1. Confirm move-in date and time in writing
2. Collect full move-in funds before handing over any keys
3. Walk through the room and common areas together, noting existing condition
4. Take dated photos with the tenant present
5. Review house rules together and answer any questions
6. Collect signed tenant agreement and signed house rules acknowledgment
7. Provide keys, WiFi password, and welcome guide
8. Follow up within 3 to 5 days to make sure everything is going well

A Word Before You Go...

Your people are out there right now looking for exactly what you are about to build. The listing you write this week could change someone's life.

Write down three local organizations you will contact this week in the notes below. Those three calls could fill your first property.

Notes

Notes

CHAPTER EIGHT

Who to Call in Your Area

This chapter might be the most immediately actionable section in this entire book. The people who will send you the most consistent, pre-qualified tenants are not on the internet looking for your listing. They're sitting in offices and community centers, actively trying to solve a housing problem for the people they serve.

Your Key Contact List

VA Offices and Veteran Service Organizations

Contact housing specialists, case managers, and social workers who work directly with veterans. Also contact VSOs like the American Legion, VFW, DAV, and local veteran-focused nonprofits.

SCRIPT

CALLING THE VA:
'Hello, I'm looking to speak with whoever handles housing assistance for veterans. My name is [Name] and I operate a professional shared housing property in [area] specifically designed to serve veterans and individuals on fixed income. My rooms are clean, affordable, and available now. I'd love to introduce myself as a resource for any veterans who may be looking for stable housing.'

Social Services and Housing Agencies

- County Department of Social Services
- Community Action Agencies
- Continuum of Care programs
- Housing Authority — which administers Section 8/HUD-VASH vouchers

Recovery Houses and Treatment Centers

Contact discharge planners or case managers at local treatment facilities, halfway houses, and recovery support organizations. Introduce yourself as a housing resource for people completing their programs.

Domestic Violence Shelters

For women's rooming houses especially, local domestic violence shelters are an excellent referral source. Women leaving shelter situations need transitional housing in a safe, structured environment.

Workforce Development Programs

Local workforce development programs serve adults in economic transition. Connect with case managers and career coaches at these programs.

Local Churches and Faith Communities

Faith communities often have active housing assistance ministries. Introduce yourself to the pastor or ministry leader who oversees social outreach. Faith community referrals often come with a built-in level of vetting.

Property Managers and Landlords

SCRIPT

CALLING A PROPERTY MANAGER:
'Hi, my name is [Name] and I operate a shared housing property in [area]. I work primarily with adults on fixed income and individuals in housing transition. I wanted to introduce myself in case you ever have an applicant who doesn't fit your property but might be a good fit for mine. Would you be open to having my contact on file for situations like that?'

Building Your Referral Pipeline

- Follow up consistently every four to six weeks even when you don't have a vacancy
- Send a simple one-page property info sheet to every contact
- Notify your network immediately when rooms open
- Treat referred tenants exceptionally well — your reputation multiplies

REAL TALK

The operators who consistently have full properties are the ones out in the community, building relationships, making calls, and showing up. This business rewards activity — and the community relationships you build in year one will serve you for a decade.

A Word Before You Go...

Every relationship you build from this chapter is a referral pipeline that runs itself. You are not just making calls — you are planting seeds that grow into a full property.

Write down one person you already know in social services, ministry, or veteran support. That person is your first referral partner. Reach out this week.

Notes

Notes

CHAPTER NINE

Legal Awareness (Not Legal Advice)

This chapter is not legal advice. Laws, ordinances, and regulations vary significantly by city, county, and state. Before you launch any shared housing business, consult with a local real estate attorney.

Zoning and Land Use

Zoning laws determine how land and buildings can be used. Most residential zones permit single-family or multi-family housing, but they may also include rules about how many unrelated adults can occupy a single-family residence. Call your city's planning or zoning department and ask directly about maximum occupancy for unrelated adults in a residential zone.

WATCH OUT

Zoning violations can result in fines, mandatory evictions, and forced closure of your operation. Thirty minutes of research before you sign a lease can save you an enormous amount of trouble later.

The Living Agreement vs. The Lease

This is the most legally significant decision you will make in this business. For rooming houses and standard shared housing — use a sublease agreement. For sober living, transitional housing, and reentry housing — use a living agreement. The difference determines your legal relationship with residents and your options if something goes wrong.

LEGAL NOTE

Never use a standard lease for sober living or transitional housing programs.
Never use a living agreement and call it a lease.
The language in your agreements must accurately reflect the nature of the relationship.
Have a local attorney review all agreements before you use them.

Fair Housing Basics

The Fair Housing Act prohibits discrimination based on race, color, national origin, religion, sex, familial status, and disability. Most states add additional protected classes. Screen all applicants using consistent, objective criteria.

Staying Compliant Without Overcomplicating It

- Verify local zoning and occupancy limits before signing any lease
- Get landlord permission to sublease in writing
- Use written tenant agreements that comply with your state's landlord-tenant law
- Follow your state's rules on security deposits
- Give proper notice before entering a tenant's room
- Follow eviction procedures exactly if you ever need to remove a tenant
- Consult an attorney before and whenever you're unsure

COACH TIP

The best time to talk to a local real estate attorney is before you sign your first lease. An hour of legal consultation — typically $150 to $350 — is one of the best investments you can make at the beginning of this business.

A Word Before You Go...

Knowledge protects what you build. You now have the knowledge — and that is not a small thing. Let it give you the confidence to move forward legally and boldly.

Write down the name of one local real estate attorney to research this week. One hour of consultation is the best investment you will make at the start of this business.

Notes

Notes

CHAPTER TEN

Common Pitfalls & How to Avoid Them

Every business has pitfalls, and shared housing is no exception. The good news is that most of the mistakes new operators make are predictable — which means they're preventable.

Pitfall #1: Skipping Tenant Screening

This is the number one mistake. The pressure to fill a room quickly can push you toward accepting the first person who shows up. Don't do it. A single bad tenant can disrupt the entire household, damage your property, stop paying rent, and take three months to remove.

WATCH OUT

Trust your gut — but don't rely on it alone. Always verify income, check references, and complete your standard screening conversation before approving anyone.

Pitfall #2: Using the Wrong Agreement Type

For operators running program-based housing — sober living, transitional, or reentry homes — using a standard lease instead of a living agreement eliminates your most important legal protection. Know your model. Use the right agreement. This is not optional.

BEGINNER MISTAKE

Treating a sober living home like a rooming house. The moment you use a standard lease with a sober living resident, you have created a landlord-tenant relationship — and you've lost the legal protections that come with the program participation model.

Pitfall #3: Poor Documentation

Every agreement, every rule, every move-in condition, and every maintenance request should be documented in writing. Keep dated photographs at move-in and move-out. Keep written records of any rule violations or warnings. Undocumented incidents become disputes.

Pitfall #4: Underpricing Your Rooms

If you price your rooms below your break-even point, you're building a charity, not a business. Research your local market and price based on your actual costs plus a sustainable margin. A business that can't sustain itself can't serve anyone.

Pitfall #5: Landlord Conflicts

Everything about your operation depends on that lease staying intact. Pay rent on time, every month, without exception. Communicate proactively about maintenance issues. Honor the terms of your lease exactly. Don't make unauthorized modifications to the property.

Pitfall #6: Cash Flow Mismanagement

Separate your business finances from your personal finances from day one. Open a dedicated business checking account. Keep a reserve fund of at least two months of operating expenses. Track every dollar in and out.

MONEY MOVE

Set up your rent collection on an automatic recurring payment system. Manual rent collection creates awkward moments when tenants are late. Automatic payments make income consistent and the conversations easier.

Pitfall #7: Operator Burnout

The solution is systems. When your cleaning system, maintenance system, communication system, and tenant screening system are all set up and running smoothly, the property manages itself for the most part. Build systems early. They protect your time and your sanity.

A Word Before You Go...

The operators who succeed are not the ones who never make mistakes — they are the ones who planned for them. You now have the plan. That puts you ahead of most.

Write down your biggest fear about this business in the notes below. Name it. Then write one way you would handle it. Fear named is fear managed.

Notes

Notes

CHAPTER ELEVEN

Scaling This Into a Real Business

What would your life look like if you had five shared housing properties running simultaneously? At a conservative average of $900 net income per property, that's $4,500 per month. Managing five properties with good systems doesn't take five times as much work as managing one. It takes maybe twice as much work — and that's only if you haven't started delegating yet.

Start Right: Master Your First Property

Before you think about property number two, make sure property number one is running smoothly. Rooms are full, systems are in place, cash flow is positive. This process typically takes three to six months from your first move-in. Use this time intentionally — document every process as if you're creating a manual for someone else to follow. Because eventually, someone else will.

Building Systems That Run Without You

Tenant Communication System

Use a single platform for all tenant communication. Set the expectation that you respond to non-urgent messages within 24 hours and urgent maintenance within the same day. This boundary protects your time while maintaining professional responsiveness.

Rent Collection System

All rent should be collected digitally on the same day each month. Use a platform that sends automatic reminders and tracks payment status. Remove emotion from this process and make it systematic.

Maintenance System

Create a simple maintenance request form that captures the issue, location, urgency, and a photo. A Google Form works perfectly. Track completion. Documented, quickly resolved maintenance builds tenant trust.

Cleaning and Turnover System

Build a relationship with a reliable cleaning professional for both regular maintenance cleaning and the deep clean required between tenants. Create a standard turnover checklist so every room reset happens consistently.

Hiring Help

At some point — typically around property number three or four — the value of your time exceeds the cost of delegating. The first hire most operators make is a property assistant or co-manager who handles day-to-day tenant communications, conducts viewings, and coordinates maintenance.

MONEY MOVE

Offer a Property Ambassador arrangement to a trusted existing tenant: in exchange for assisting with viewings and being a first point of contact for minor issues, they receive a $75–$150/month rent reduction. This costs you very little and adds genuine operational capacity.

Income Projection

Properties	Avg. Net/Month	Monthly Net	Annual Net
1	$900	$900	$10,800
2	$950	$1,900	$22,800
3	$1,000	$3,000	$36,000
5	$1,050	$5,250	$63,000
8	$1,100	$8,800	$105,600

Start with one. Do it right. Build the systems. Then take the next step. And the next. That's not a theory — that's a business plan.

A Word Before You Go...

You are not building a side hustle. You are building a legacy — one property at a time. God does not give vision without provision. Trust the process.

Write down what three properties would mean for your life financially. Let that number motivate everything that comes next.

Notes

Notes

CHAPTER TWELVE

Beginner FAQ: 35 Real Questions, Real Answers

This chapter is for every question you've been holding in your head since chapter one. Answered plainly, without hedging or corporate speak. Let's go.

Q1: Do I need a real estate license?
No. You are leasing a property as a tenant and subleasing individual rooms. This is a business activity that does not require a real estate license.

Q2: How much money do I need to get started?
Most people get started with $3,000 to $7,000. This covers your first month's rent, security deposit to the landlord, and the cost of furnishing the property.

Q3: What if my credit isn't perfect?
Credit matters less here than you think. You're approaching private landlords, not banks. Your plan and your professionalism do more work than your credit score.

Q4: What if the landlord says no?
Move on to the next one. You only need one yes to get started, and every conversation makes you better at the next one.

Q5: Can I do this if I have a full-time job?
Yes. The time-intensive period is the first 60 to 90 days. Once the property is running smoothly, ongoing management typically requires 5 to 10 hours per week.

Q6: What if a tenant doesn't pay rent?

Start your formal process immediately. Send a written notice on day one of non-payment. Follow your state's legal process for late rent notices and, if necessary, eviction.

Q7: What is the difference between a lease and a living agreement?

A lease creates a landlord-tenant relationship governed by state landlord-tenant law. A living agreement creates a program operator-participant relationship. For sober living, transitional housing, and reentry housing — always use a living agreement. See the Housing Models Defined section for the complete breakdown.

Q8: What is reentry housing?

Reentry housing is transitional housing for adults coming out of incarceration. It is included as Bonus Chapter Eight in this updated edition. See that chapter for the complete breakdown.

Q9: Is this legal in my city?

Rental arbitrage is legal in most cities, but zoning, occupancy limits, and local ordinances vary. Research your city's rules, check your lease agreement, and consult a local attorney before launching.

Q10: What if I can't fill all the rooms right away?

Budget for it. Plan to cover at least 60 days of lease costs from your own pocket as you fill rooms for the first time.

Q11: Do my tenants need to sign a lease?

For rooming houses — yes, a sublease agreement. For sober living, transitional, and reentry housing — a living agreement, not a lease.

Q12: What is ALF and is it the same as what I'm doing?

ALF stands for Assisted Living Facility — a licensed, regulated care setting for adults who need help with daily activities. This is completely different from what we teach. You are a housing provider, not a care provider. No ALF license is needed for any model in this book.

Q13: What is the difference between a licensed and unlicensed group home?

A licensed group home requires state licensing, professional staff, and ongoing regulatory compliance — it provides clinical care. An unlicensed group home provides housing to self-sufficient adults with no clinical oversight required. See the Housing Models Defined section.

Q14: What is transitional housing?

Temporary, structured housing designed to help people move from a crisis situation toward stable independent living. It is program-based, uses living agreements, and serves people in transition from treatment, domestic violence situations, incarceration, or other crisis circumstances.

Q15: Can I run this as a woman?

Absolutely — and in many cases being a woman operator is an advantage. You often communicate more thoughtfully, establish clearer household culture, and run women's housing with an authenticity that male operators simply can't match.

Q16: What happens if my landlord sells the property?

Your lease typically transfers to the new owner — meaning the new landlord must honor the remaining term of your existing lease. This is why having a solid, written lease agreement matters.

Q17: Should I form an LLC?

Many operators eventually do, for liability protection and cleaner business finances. Discuss with a local attorney and accountant early in your business.

Q18: Can I accept housing vouchers?

Yes, in most states. Taking housing vouchers connects you to a pre-qualified tenant population with guaranteed partial rent payment from the government.

Q19: How many properties can one person manage?

With good systems, most solo operators can manage two to four properties comfortably. Beyond that, a part-time property assistant is typically needed.

Q20: What's the hardest part of this business?

For most operators, the hardest part is the beginning — finding the first property and having the confidence to have the landlord conversation. Once that first property is running, the second is significantly easier.

Q21: Can I do this in a small city?

Yes — and in some ways small cities are better. Less competition, lower lease costs, and the same demand for affordable shared housing.

Q22: What if a tenant damages the property?

Document all damage with dated photos during move-out inspection. Apply the security deposit against repair costs.

Q23: How do I get furniture cheap?

Facebook Marketplace is your best friend. You can furnish an entire room for $150 to $300 if you're patient and strategic.

Q24: How do I handle taxes?

This is a conversation for a CPA or tax professional. Your rental income is taxable, and your business expenses are generally deductible. Track every expense carefully.

Q25: What makes reentry housing different from other transitional housing?

Reentry housing specifically serves adults coming out of incarceration. It involves specific legal considerations around background checks, fair chance housing laws, and parole compliance requirements.

Q26: Is this passive income?

Not at first. The first 60 to 90 days are active. After that, with good systems, it shifts to semi-passive — 5 to 10 hours per week. With multiple properties and help, it can approach true passive income.

Q27: How fast can I start making money?
30 to 60 days from reading this book to your first tenant moved in is realistic if you move with intention. The 30-Day Action Plan in the bonus section maps it out week by week.

Q28: Do I need a website?
Not to start. Your listings on Furnished Finder, Facebook Marketplace, and Craigslist, combined with community referral relationships, will fill rooms without a website.

Q29: What if two tenants have a conflict?
Facilitate, don't adjudicate. Bring both parties together, let each express their concern, and establish clear expectations going forward based on the house rules.

Q30: Can I start with a 3-bedroom property?
Yes — a 3-bedroom house can generate income and teach you the model with lower initial cost and complexity. Many successful operators started small and used that experience to fund a larger second property.

Q31: Is this recession-proof?
It's more recession-resistant than most businesses. Demand for affordable housing increases in economic downturns. Maintaining financial reserves is always wise regardless.

Q32: What if I decide this isn't for me after I've started?
Honor your lease obligations. Give proper notice to all parties. Exit the lease at its natural end point if possible. This is why negotiating shorter initial lease terms when starting out makes sense.

Q33: How do I protect myself if a tenant refuses to leave?
Follow the legal eviction process in your state exactly. Do not skip steps or take shortcuts. Consult an attorney before taking any action if you're unsure.

Q34: What's the best model to start with?

Most beginners do best starting with a mid-sized house targeting either veterans and fixed-income adults or general population working adults. Choose the model that aligns best with your local market and personal strengths.

A Word Before You Go...

Every question you had when you opened this book — you now have the answer. You came in as a beginner. You are leaving as someone who knows exactly what to do next.

Write down the date you will sign your first lease in the notes below. Put it in writing. Make it real. That date is the beginning of everything.

Notes

Notes

BONUS 1: Sample Landlord Script (Word-for-Word)

Use this script as a starting point for your landlord conversation. Adapt it to your voice and your specific model. The goal is not to memorize it word-for-word — it's to internalize the structure and key points so you can speak to it naturally.

SCRIPT

INITIAL INQUIRY (by phone or email):
'Hi, I'm calling about the 5-bedroom house you have listed at [address]. My name is [Your Name] and I'm interested in arranging a viewing. I do want to mention upfront that I operate a professional shared housing business — I lease properties and manage them as organized shared housing for pre-screened adult tenants. I'd love to share more about how that arrangement works if you're open to it.'

DURING OR AFTER THE TOUR:
'I'd like to tell you a bit more about what I do, because I want to be completely transparent with you. I run a professional shared housing operation. I lease properties, furnish them to a good standard, and rent individual rooms to pre-screened adults. What that means for you is one reliable tenant — me — who pays rent on time every month. I handle all the day-to-day management. I'm looking to sign a 12-to-24-month lease, pay first month and deposit upfront, and operate the property to a high standard. The only thing I need from you is written permission to sublease individual rooms. Would you be open to talking through that arrangement?'

IF THEY ASK ABOUT LIABILITY:
'As the primary tenant on the lease, I'm your single point of accountability. You're not dealing with five different tenants — you're dealing with me. My sub-tenants have agreements with me, not with you directly.'

IF THEY ASK ABOUT PROPERTY CONDITION:
'I do a documented inspection with photos at every tenant move-in and move-out. I have a maintenance budget for minor repairs. And I'm actually more attentive to the property day-to-day than most single tenants because I'm checking in regularly as part of managing the household. I'm happy to provide a reference from my current landlord if that would be helpful.'

BONUS 2: Sample Tenant Agreement Outline

This outline covers the essential elements of your subtenant agreement. Use this as a guide when working with your attorney to create a legally compliant document for your state. This is an outline only — not a finished legal document.

1. Parties

Full legal names of operator and tenant. Property address and specific room number or description.

2. Term

Start date and end date, or month-to-month designation. Notice required to terminate — typically 30 days for month-to-month.

3. Rent

Monthly rental amount. Due date (e.g., 1st of each month). Acceptable payment methods. Late fee amount and when it applies.

4. Security Deposit

Amount collected. Conditions under which it may be withheld. Timeline for return per state law.

5. Utilities and Services Included

Explicit list of what is included in the monthly rate: electric, gas, water, internet, etc.

6. Use of Premises

Room is for residential use only by the named tenant. Guest policy per house rules. No further subletting.

7. House Rules

House Rules document attached and incorporated by reference. Tenant acknowledges receipt and agreement.

8. Maintenance and Repairs

Tenant responsibility to report issues promptly. Operator responsibility to address legitimate maintenance within reasonable timeframe.

9. Entry Notice

Operator's right to enter with proper notice — typically 24–48 hours per state law.

10. Termination for Cause

Grounds for early termination by operator. Notice required. Legal eviction process will be followed if necessary.

11. Move-Out Condition

Room returned in same condition as received, less normal wear. Move-out inspection and documentation process.

12. Signatures

Date, signature, and printed name of both operator and tenant.

WATCH OUT

Have a local attorney review your actual tenant agreement before you use it. Landlord-tenant law is state-specific, and an agreement missing required disclosures in your state could create legal problems.

BONUS 3: Sample House Rules Document

Adapt these rules to your specific property and model. Post them in a common area and provide a signed copy to every tenant at move-in.

HOUSEHOLD RULES & EXPECTATIONS

Welcome to your new home. This house is a shared living community, and the rules below exist to ensure that every resident — including you — has a clean, peaceful, and respectful place to live.

RENT PAYMENT

- Rent is due on the 1st of each month
- A late fee of $[amount] applies after the [5th] of the month
- Accepted payment methods: [list your methods]

QUIET HOURS

- Weekdays: 10:00 PM to 7:00 AM
- Weekends: 11:00 PM to 8:00 AM

GUESTS

- Guests welcome during daytime and early evening hours (before 10:00 PM weekdays)
- No overnight guests without prior written approval from management
- Residents fully responsible for behavior of their guests

KITCHEN

- Clean up after every use. No dishes in the sink for more than 24 hours.
- Label your food in the shared refrigerator
- Do not use food that is not yours

SUBSTANCES

- No illegal substances anywhere on the property at any time

- Alcohol policy: [insert your policy based on your model]

RESPECT AND CONDUCT

- Treat all housemates with courtesy and respect at all times
- No harassment, intimidation, threatening behavior, or violence of any kind
- Disputes between residents should be brought to management's attention

MOVE-OUT

- Provide [30] days written notice before vacating
- Return your room in the same condition as received, less normal wear
- A move-out inspection will be conducted and documented with photos

RESIDENT ACKNOWLEDGMENT

I have read, understood, and agree to comply with all house rules listed above. I understand that violations of these rules may result in a formal warning, lease violation notice, or termination of my tenancy depending on severity.

Resident Name (Print):

____

Resident Signature: ___________________________________
Date: ____________

Management Signature:
___________________________________ Date:
____

BONUS 4: Startup Checklist

PHASE 1: FOUNDATION

- Decide on your target model based on market research
- Research your local market — comparable room rates, demand, competition
- Research your city/county zoning and occupancy rules
- Consult a local real estate attorney
- Open a dedicated business bank account
- Determine your startup budget and confirm available funds

PHASE 2: FINDING AND SECURING A PROPERTY

- Begin searching: Zillow, Craigslist, Facebook Marketplace
- Create a property evaluation criteria list
- Tour at least 5 properties before signing anything
- Have the rental arbitrage conversation with at least 3 landlords
- Negotiate lease terms and subletting addendum
- Sign master lease and pay first month plus deposit

PHASE 3: PROPERTY SETUP

- Deep clean the property (hire professional for first setup)
- Document all rooms with dated photos before any furniture arrives
- Set up utilities in your name: electric, gas, water, internet
- Purchase and install bedroom furniture
- Furnish common areas: kitchen, living room, bathrooms
- Install locks on bedroom doors
- Create and print House Rules document
- Set up maintenance request system and rent collection system

PHASE 4: MARKETING AND FILLING

- Take professional-quality listing photos of every room and common area
- Create listings on Furnished Finder, Facebook Marketplace, Craigslist
- Contact VA office, social service agencies, recovery programs, shelters
- Begin scheduling viewings for interested applicants

PHASE 5: TENANT SELECTION AND MOVE-IN

- Conduct screening conversation with every applicant
- Complete income verification for every approved applicant
- Check at least one reference per applicant
- Collect signed agreements and move-in funds before handing keys
- Conduct move-in walkthrough and document with photos
- Follow up within 3 to 5 days after move-in

BONUS 5: Your First 30-Day Action Plan

WEEK 1: Education and Research

- Complete this entire book
- Research your local market — search Craigslist, Facebook, and Furnished Finder for comparable rooms
- Call your city's planning department and ask about zoning and occupancy rules
- Schedule a consultation with a local real estate attorney
- Open a business bank account
- Decide on your target model based on market research

WEEK 2: Preparation and Property Search

- Create your landlord pitch and practice it out loud at least three times
- Begin touring properties — aim for at least 3 viewings this week
- Have the rental arbitrage conversation with at least one landlord
- Draft your tenant agreement template with attorney input
- Draft your house rules document

WEEK 3: Landlord Conversations and Lease Negotiation

- Continue touring and having landlord conversations — aim for 5 or more total
- Follow up with any landlords who seemed interested from week 2
- Negotiate lease terms and subletting addendum if ready
- Begin your community outreach calls: VA office, social services, recovery programs

WEEK 4: Setup and Pre-Launch

- Set up utilities in your name if lease is signed
- Document all rooms with photos before furniture arrives
- Purchase and set up furniture using your budget and Facebook Marketplace strategy
- Take final listing photos once property is furnished and ready
- Publish listings and begin scheduling first viewings

- Follow up with every community contact from week 3

COACH TIP

Don't wait until everything is perfect to start. Progress beats perfection every single time in this business. Start, learn, adjust, repeat.

BONUS 6: Sample Monthly Income Breakdown

Here are three different scenarios — small, medium, and portfolio — so you can see what the actual numbers look like across different property sizes and configurations.

SCENARIO A: Starter Property — 4-Bedroom House

Item	Monthly Amount
Master lease rent	-$1,600
Utilities (electric, gas, water, internet)	-$305
Supplies & maintenance reserve	-$220
8 beds x $425/bed/month	+$3,400
GROSS INCOME	$3,400
TOTAL EXPENSES	$2,125
NET MONTHLY PROFIT	$1,275

SCENARIO B: Mid-Size — 5-Bedroom VA Model

Item	Monthly Amount
Master lease rent	-$2,000
Utilities	-$360
Supplies & maintenance reserve	-$280
8 beds x $475/bed/month	+$3,800
GROSS INCOME	$3,800
TOTAL EXPENSES	$2,640
NET MONTHLY PROFIT	$1,160

SCENARIO C: Three-Property Portfolio

Property	Gross Income	Expenses	Net Income
Property 1 (4-bed, established)	$3,400	$2,100	$1,300
Property 2 (5-bed, VA model)	$4,200	$2,750	$1,450
Property 3 (5-bed, co-living)	$4,500	$2,900	$1,600
TOTALS	$12,100	$7,750	$4,350

REAL TALK

These numbers assume full or near-full occupancy. Real operations will have occasional vacancies, unexpected repairs, and months that underperform. The operators who sustain this income long-term are the ones who plan for imperfection, maintain their reserves, and keep improving their systems.

BONUS 7: Sober Living Homes — The High-Impact, High-Profit Model

A sober living home is a shared housing environment for adults who are in recovery from substance use disorders. These are people who have completed or are actively engaged in a treatment program and who need a structured, substance-free environment to continue building their recovery. You are not providing treatment. You are providing housing and structure.

The Living Agreement vs. The Lease

This is the most important legal distinction in this model. Standard shared housing uses a lease — creating a landlord-tenant relationship. Sober living uses a living agreement — creating a program operator-participant relationship. If someone relapses and violates the core condition of their program agreement, you are dis-enrolling a program participant — not evicting a tenant. One word difference. Completely different legal situation.

WATCH OUT

Never use a standard lease for sober living operations. The living agreement is the legal foundation that makes this model work. Have an attorney review yours before use.

Core Program Requirements

- Complete abstinence from alcohol and all non-prescribed drugs
- Random drug and alcohol testing — consent required in living agreement
- Minimum meeting attendance — typically 3 to 5 per week
- Weekly house meetings and household responsibilities
- Curfew compliance
- Active employment or programming within a defined period
- On-time payment of program fees

Curfew Structure

Resident Status	Typical Curfew
New residents (first 30 days)	10:00 PM weekdays / 11:00 PM weekends
30–90 days, good standing	11:00 PM weekdays / Midnight weekends
90+ days, excellent standing	Midnight weekdays / 1:00 AM weekends
Late work schedule (documented)	Modified with House Manager approval

Grounds for Removal

Immediate Removal

- Use of alcohol or non-prescribed drugs — confirmed by test or witnessed
- Bringing substances onto the property
- Violence or threats of violence
- Sexual misconduct or harassment
- Tampering with a drug test

Process-Based Removal

- Repeated curfew violations
- Failure to attend required meetings without documentation
- Non-payment of program fees beyond grace period
- Repeated guest policy violations

Income Breakdown

Item	Monthly Amount
Master lease (5-bed house)	-$2,000
Utilities	-$420
Drug testing supplies	-$90
Cleaning supplies & staples	-$100
House Manager stipend	-$250

Item	Monthly Amount
Maintenance reserve	-$200
8 beds x $875/month program fee	+$7,000
TOTAL EXPENSES	$3,060
NET MONTHLY PROFIT	$3,940

NUMBERS BREAKDOWN

THREE-HOME PORTFOLIO PROJECTION:
Home 1 (established, full): $3,940/month net
Home 2 (6 months old, 90% occupancy): $3,300/month net
Home 3 (new, 75% occupancy): $2,600/month net
COMBINED MONTHLY NET: $9,840
COMBINED ANNUAL NET: $118,080

Run it right. Run it with heart. And run it like the business it is.

BONUS 8: The Reentry Housing Model — Serving Those Starting Over

This bonus chapter addresses one of the most urgently needed and most underserved housing models in America. The reentry housing model provides structured transitional housing for adults coming out of incarceration — a daily, year-round, institutionally-supported need that exists in every city in the country.

The Crisis Nobody Talks About

Every single day, people walk out of correctional facilities across this country. They served their time. They are ready to rebuild. And they walk out the door with sometimes nothing more than a bus ticket and a garbage bag of personal belongings.

Stable housing in the first 72 hours after release is one of the single greatest predictors of whether someone successfully reintegrates into society or ends up back in the system. Seventy-two hours. Three days. That window is everything.

Without a stable address in those first three days, a person leaving incarceration cannot fulfill parole requirements, apply for jobs, access government benefits, open a bank account, or do any of the practical things that rebuilding a life requires.

REAL TALK

The United States releases approximately 600,000 people from state and federal prisons every year.

An additional 10 million people cycle through local jails annually.

An estimated 50,000+ people are released from incarceration into homelessness every year.

Studies consistently show stable housing in the reentry period is one of the strongest predictors of successful reintegration.

The demand for quality reentry housing is not a niche. It is a national emergency.

Who Your Residents Are

Your residents in a reentry home are adults who have been released from a correctional facility. They may be on parole or probation.

Most people who have been incarcerated were convicted of non-violent offenses. They are human beings in a critical transition — and they are often extraordinarily motivated to succeed precisely because they know what failure looks like.

COACH TIP

The residents who thrive in reentry housing typically have specific goals, honest self-reflection about their past, and a clear understanding of what they need to do differently. Those indicators predict success far better than the nature of the offense.

The 72-Hour Window

When someone is released from incarceration, the clock starts immediately. Parole and probation officers typically require clients to report within 24 to 48 hours of release. That reporting requires a home address. Without one, the person is technically in violation of their supervision conditions before they've had a chance to comply.

The reentry housing provider who can offer a clean, safe room on day one of release is providing the foundation that makes every other part of reintegration possible. That is an extraordinarily valuable service — and it is chronically undersupplied.

MONEY MOVE

Contact your local parole and probation offices before you open. Ask specifically about their process for placing newly released individuals in housing. In many jurisdictions, parole officers have a list of approved housing providers they refer their clients to immediately upon release. Getting on that list is one of the most powerful business development moves you can make.

Legal Considerations

Background Check Policies

You are housing people with criminal records by definition. Understand which conviction types your program is equipped to serve. Residency restrictions for registered sex offenders vary dramatically by state and municipality — research your property's address in relation to applicable restrictions before accepting any resident. Never accept a resident if their placement would violate their registration conditions.

LEGAL NOTE

Residency restrictions for registered sex offenders vary dramatically by state and municipality.

Before accepting any resident, research your property's address in relation to applicable restrictions.

Consult your local attorney and state's sex offender registry rules before developing your intake policy.

Fair Chance Housing Laws

Fair chance housing laws restrict when and how landlords can use criminal history information in rental decisions. These laws vary significantly by state and city. Research your city's specific laws before developing your intake and screening process. Consult an attorney about how these laws apply to your specific program model.

Parole and Probation Compliance

Many of your residents will be under active supervision. Parole officers may conduct home visits. Your residents may have curfews set by their supervision conditions that are stricter than your house curfew — always honor the strictest applicable curfew. Build relationships with parole and probation officers who supervise your residents.

The Referral Pipeline

Parole Officers

Parole officers are required to verify their clients have stable housing. Many parole offices maintain lists of approved housing providers. Getting on that list can produce a steady stream of referrals from day one.

SCRIPT

CALLING A PAROLE OFFICE:
'Hello, my name is [Your Name] and I operate a professional reentry housing program in [city/area]. We provide structured, clean, affordable transitional housing specifically for adults coming out of incarceration.

I wanted to introduce myself because I know finding quality housing for newly released individuals is often one of the most urgent challenges you face. I have [X] beds available, we operate 24/7, and we can often accommodate placements with very short notice.

I'd love to give you my information and walk you through our program so you know exactly what your clients would be walking into. Is this a good time?'

Other Key Referral Sources

- Reentry organizations and nonprofits — actively looking for quality housing partners
- Correctional facility pre-release programs — begin housing placement before release
- Drug courts and diversion courts — place participants in housing as part of program requirements
- Faith communities with prison ministry — active relationships with people coming out of incarceration
- Workforce development programs — need housing resources for their clients

Program Structure

Core Requirements

- Compliance with all parole or probation conditions
- Active job search or employment within a defined period after move-in
- Curfew compliance — honor both house curfew and supervision-imposed curfew
- No illegal substances on the property
- Household responsibilities and regular house meetings

- On-time payment of program fees
- Honest communication about supervision status changes

Curfew Structure

Resident Status	House Curfew	Note
New residents (first 30 days)	10:00 PM all nights	Critical stability window
30–90 days, good standing	11:00 PM weekdays / Midnight weekends	Gradual increase
90+ days, excellent standing	Midnight weekdays / 1:00 AM weekends	Reward compliance
Parole/probation curfew applies	Earlier of supervision or house curfew	Supervision always first

Income Breakdown

Item	Monthly Amount
Master lease (5-bed house)	-$2,000
Utilities	-$380
Supplies & household staples	-$120
House Manager stipend	-$300
Maintenance reserve	-$200
Admin & miscellaneous	-$100
8 beds x $650/month program fee	+$5,200
TOTAL EXPENSES	$3,100
NET MONTHLY PROFIT	$2,100

MONEY MOVE

Many reentry residents qualify for government assistance that can help with housing costs:

SNAP – frees up income for housing

Medicaid – reduces healthcare costs

State reentry assistance programs – some states have specific housing assistance

Second Chance Act grants – federal funding that supports reentry housing programs

Connect your residents with benefits navigators at reentry organizations.

Funding Opportunities

- Second Chance Act funding: Federal grants that support reentry programs, including housing
- State criminal justice reform funding: Many states fund programs that reduce recidivism
- Community Development Block Grants (CDBG): Federal funding that supports affordable housing
- Private foundations focused on criminal justice reform and housing
- Corporate partnerships with companies committed to fair chance hiring

REAL TALK

Reentry housing is not the easiest model in this book to operate.

It requires more intentional structure, more active management, and more patience.

But the operators who get it right create something remarkable – businesses that are financially strong and socially transformative.

They create homes where people rebuild their lives.

And they build reputations that open doors no other housing model produces.

If this model is calling to you, it is worth the extra effort.

The world desperately needs more people willing to answer that call.

Every person who walks out of a correctional facility
is somebody's child. Somebody's parent. Somebody's hope.

Build the bridge. Open the door. Change the outcome.

You Now Have Everything You Need

The only thing left is to begin.

You've just read the most complete beginner's guide to shared housing income available anywhere — updated to include every model from standard rooming houses to the specialized program models that generate the highest income and the deepest community impact.

Start with one conversation. One property. One tenant. And build from there.

You've got this.

— Kelly Janine Joyner